Mycology

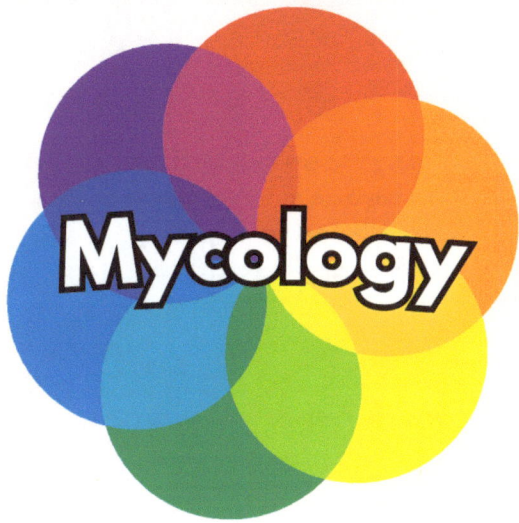

Book of
COLORS
A Rainbow of Fungi

AO PRESS

Jessica Lee Anderson

Paperback ISBN: 978-1-964078-29-8

To Angela, Damon, and Olive, thank you for your friendship and for sharing your love of mushrooms with us! - JLA

Photo credits, left to right, top to bottom: Front cover (anemone stinkhorn): Karin de Mamiel; Interior cover (oyster mushrooms): chengyuzheng; Copyright page (shimeji mushrooms): y-studio; Dedication page: Fotografiecor; p. 4: squirrel77, anytka, Erica Bandin; p. 5: engabito, Stephen Caterall, digoarpi; p. 6: Lukas Jonaitis, luamduan, fotoco-istock; 7: Maria Ogrzewalska, HHelene, nksanthoshi; p. 8: Karen H. Black, pamela_d_mcadams, ezgi; p. 9: chengyuzheng, weinkoetz, laurik; p. 10: Elena_P, tomasztc, Marcine Majdanski; p. 11: weinkoetz, Andre Muller, Birute; p. 12: randimal, IainStych, Wirestock; p. 13: Ian_Redding, Wirestock, Illuvis; p. 14: Kramar, Machacekcz, jojoo64; p. 15: _AleMasche72, AlbyDeTweede, Karen H. Black; p. 16: Karen H. Black, PlazacCamerman, weinkoetz; p. 17: Jennifer Gauld, nickkurzenko, Claudia Solari; p. 18: Araleboy, weinkoetz, Acrylic Asylum Art; p. 19: rainmax, Christi Nistor, Gerald Corsi; p. 20: AlbyDeTweede, UD10671, szjeno091980; p. 21: Mantonature, teen00000, Pete_Flyer; p. 22: Alexander62, fotoco-istock, Diana Trac; p. 23: Henrik_L, Olgaorly, Maura1; p. 24: Liudmya Liudmya, Fantastic Geographic, DutchlightNetherlands; p. 25: euapun, Savany, Maria Gawne; p. 26: weinkoetz, Wirestock; p. 27: undefined undefined, danlogan, cmtyers; p. 28: digoarpi, NickRH, Saschasnowstorm; p. 29: Nicole Gilbo, weinkoetz, fotoco-istock; p. 30: key05, doulos, Billion Photos; p. 31: OndrejVladyka, juv, Surdu Horia; p. 32: empire331, WDnetStudio, randimal; p. 33: empire331, adrianam13, p. PlazacCamerman; 34: Michael Anderson; Back cover (caterpillar fungus): chengyuzheng

This Book Belongs to:

_____

Mycology is the study of fungi (plural for fungus).

Fly agaric mushroom

Red

Fly agaric mushrooms

Bleeding tooth mushroom

Molds, yeasts, and mushrooms are all types of fungi.

Anemone stinkhorn

Red

Red hairy cup

Fungi species come in all shapes, colors, and sizes.

Scarlet elf cup

Red cage

Orange

Push pin slime mold

Caterpillar fungus

Researchers estimate there are over two million species of fungi!

Jack-o'-lantern mushrooms

Orange

Orange slime mold

Orange peel fungus

Orange mycena

Scientists are continuing to discover new species and learn more about fungi.

Yellow

Coral fungus

Nutritional yeast

Fungi may look like plants, but they don't make their own food. Fungi have their own kingdom.

Yellow jelly fungus

Yellow

Yellow brain

Butter waxcap

Dog vomit slime mold

Fungi feed on nutrients from other organisms (such as dead and dying plants).

Green

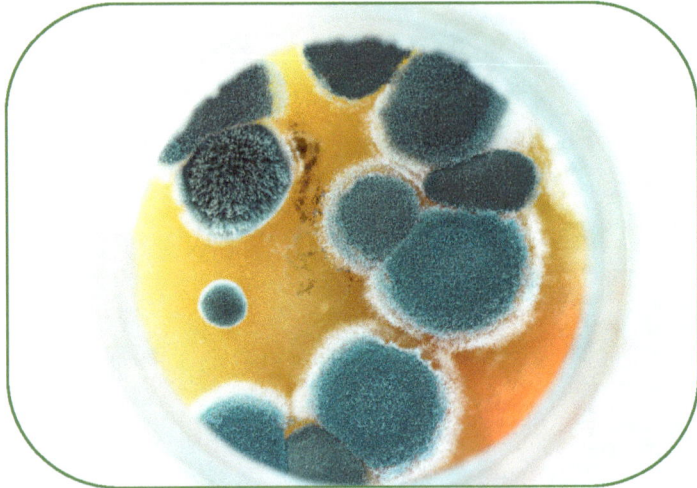

Green mold (growing in petri dish)

Green-cracking russula

Fungi play an important role in the environment and are vital to ecosystems.

Hoof fungus

Green

Olive oysterling

Green elfcup

Verdigris agaric

Many fungi are decomposers— they break down organic matter and release nutrients in the soil and air.

Blue

While certain mushrooms can be dangerous if eaten, many kinds are safe and an important source of food.

Blue tooth fungus

Blue fungus

Aniseed funnel

Blue

Green elf cup

Molds and yeasts can be used to make products like bread, cheese, beer, wine, and soy sauce.

Blue pinkgills

Pixie's parasol

Purple

Several types of mushrooms, molds, and yeasts are used to make medicines.

Purple edge bonnet

Wood blewit

Amethyst deceiver

Purple

Violet webcap

Some fungi naturally produce antibiotics like penicillin, useful for killing bacteria and fighting infections.

Hanging slime mold

Violet coral fungus

Pink

Coral fungus

Latticed stinkhorn

Fungi can be found everywhere—in the soil, in the air, and even inside living organisms (including you)!

Pink waxcap

Pink

Pink oyster mushrooms

Most fungi found on the skin and in the guts of humans are harmless and even have health benefits.

Wolf's milk slime mold

Pink slime mold

17

Black

Black mold

Velvety earth tongue

Some fungi species produce mycotoxins, toxic substances that can cause illness.

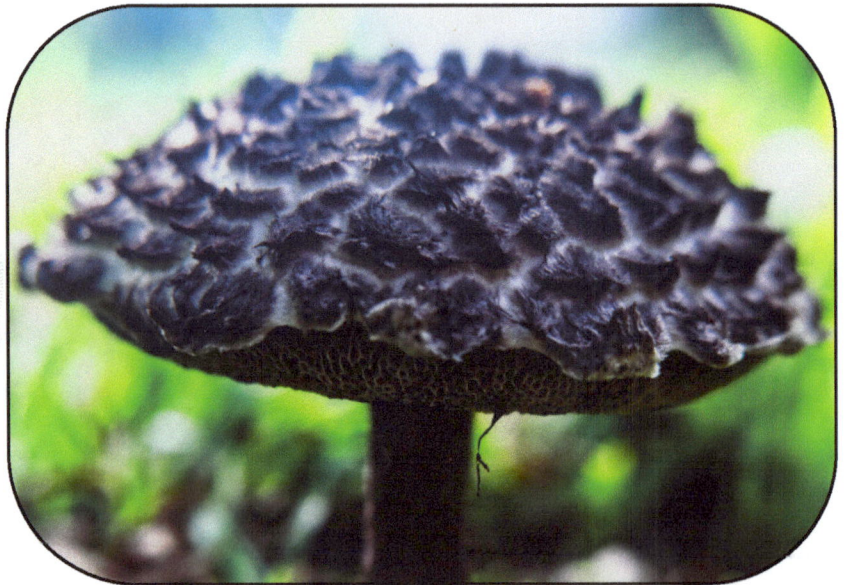

Old man of the woods

Black

Black trumpet mushrooms

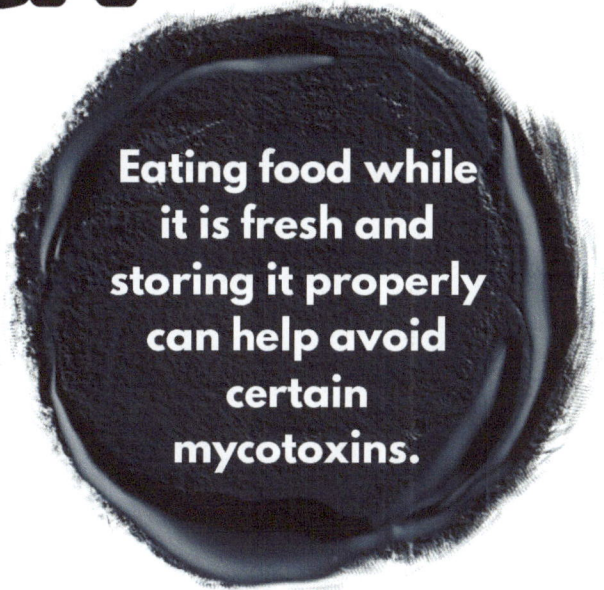

Eating food while it is fresh and storing it properly can help avoid certain mycotoxins.

Black truffles

Black jelly roll

White

Lion's mane mushroom

Oyster mushrooms

The parts of mushrooms that are above ground (like caps and stems that are eaten in some species) are called fruiting bodies.

White button mushrooms

White

White saddle mushrooms

Enoki mushrooms

Giant puffball mushrooms

Fruiting bodies produce spores that allow fungi to reproduce and spread.

Gray

Deer mushroom

Ashen chanterelle

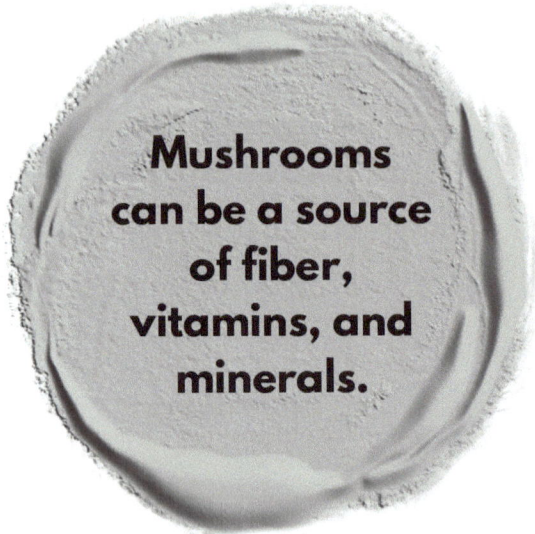

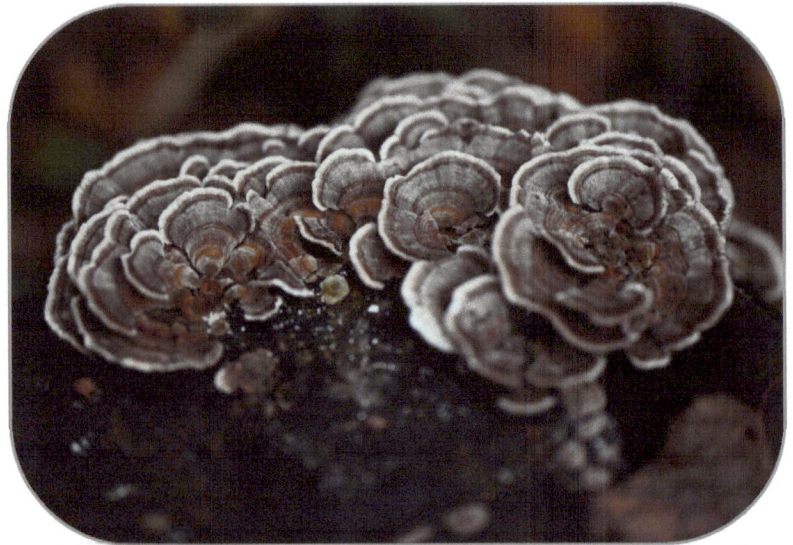

Mushrooms can be a source of fiber, vitamins, and minerals.

Turkey tail mushrooms

Gray

Grey faslebolete

Oyster mushrooms

Black morels

Some people call mushrooms that can't be eaten toadstools.

Brown

Chaga mushroom pieces

Turkey tail mushrooms

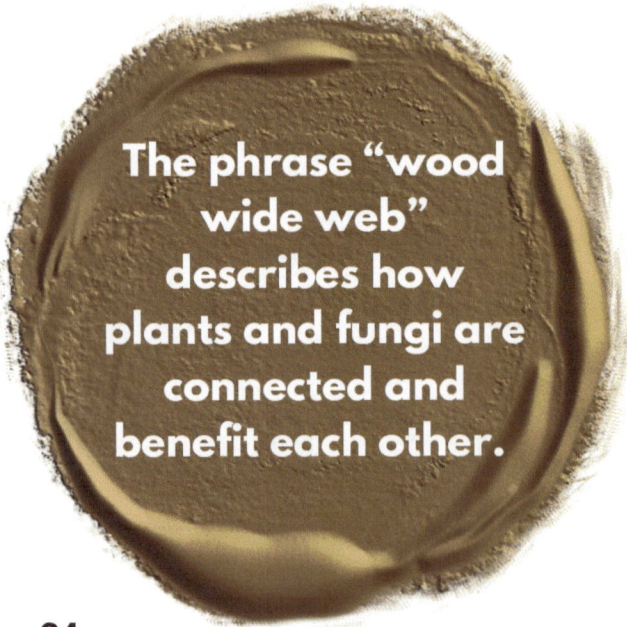

The phrase "wood wide web" describes how plants and fungi are connected and benefit each other.

Honey fungus

Brown

Maitake mushrooms

Dry yeast

Fungi is grown and eaten around the globe and is also being studied to create a natural source of fuel.

Reishi mushrooms

COLOR Combinations

Can you describe the colors and patterns of these "bleeding" fungi species?

Mealy tooth

Rosy veincap

Rosy veincap

COLOR Combinations

Grass oysterling

How are these fungi similar and different when it comes to colors, shapes, and patterns?

Chicken of the woods

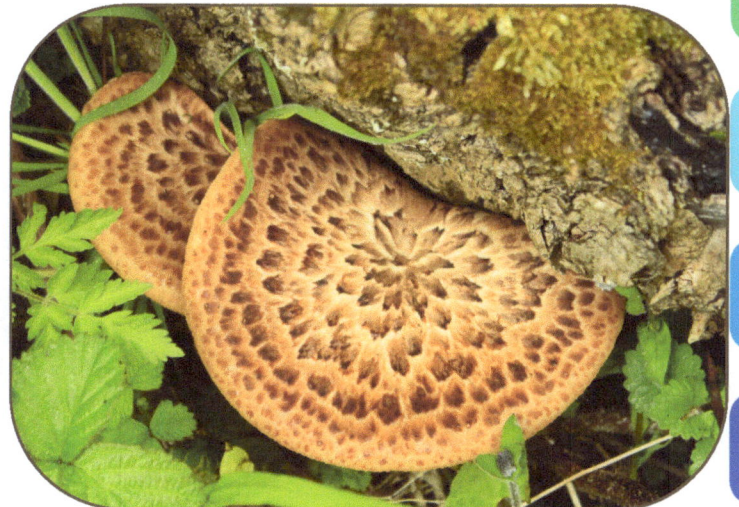

Dryad's saddle mushrooms

COLOR Combinations

Can you describe these colors and patterns?

Turkey tail mushrooms

Turkey tail mushrooms

Turkey tail mushrooms

COLOR Combinations

Pretzel slime mold

How are these fungi similar and different when it comes to colors, shapes, and patterns?

Scarlet waxcap

Golden chanterelle

COLOR Combinations

Shitake mushroom

Morel mushrooms

What are some colors and features you notice about these edible mushrooms?

Cremini mushrooms (baby bella)

COLOR Combinations

Fly agaric mushroom

How are these mushrooms similar and different when it comes to colors, shapes, and patterns?

Fly agaric mushrooms

Fly agaric mushrooms

COLOR Combinations

Caesar's mushroom (young)

Penny bun

What are some similarities and differences you observe in the colors and features of these mushrooms?

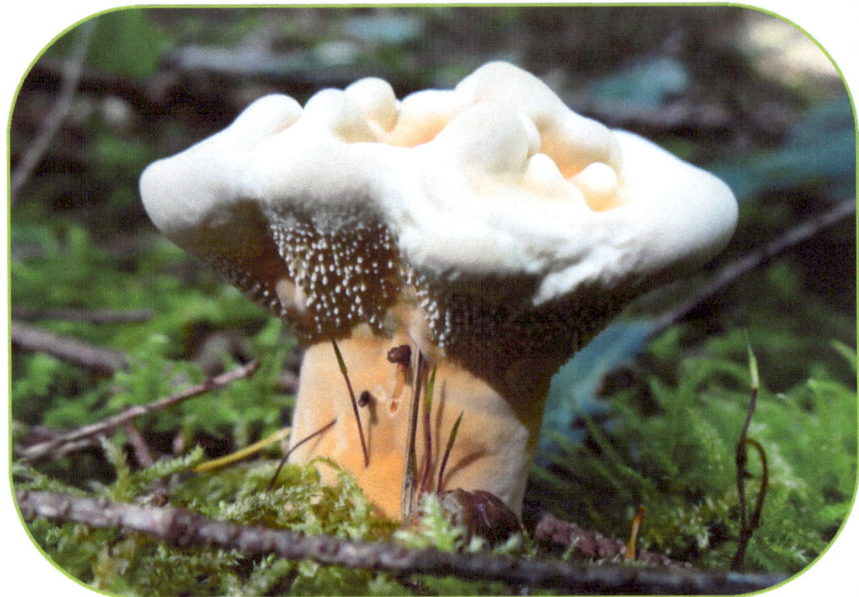
Orange spine mushroom

COLOR Combinations

Bloody brittlegill

What are the colors, shapes, and physical properties of the mushrooms? How are they the same or different?

Green-cracking russula

Pinwheel mushrooms

Jessica Lee Anderson is an award-winning author of over 75 books for young readers including the NAOMI NASH chapter book series. Jessica loves spending time in nature and exploring the outdoors with her husband, Michael, and their daughter, Ava! Jessica loves finding colorful birds near her home in Austin, Texas. You can learn more about Jessica by visiting www.jessicaleeanderson.com.

Check out these other books:

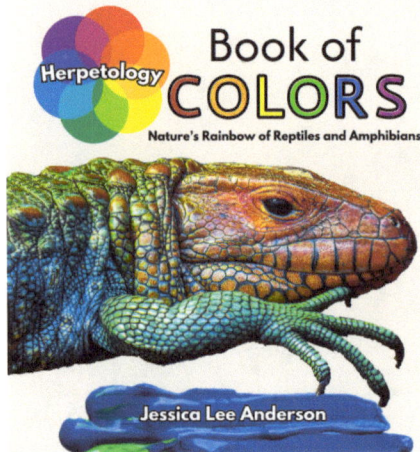

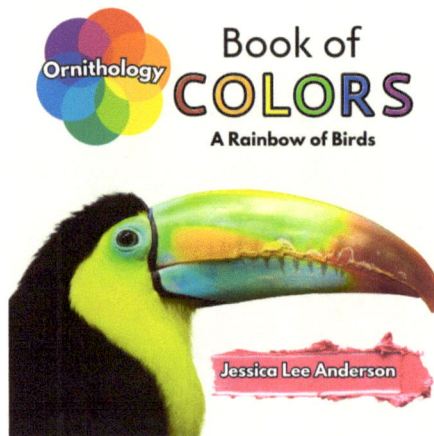

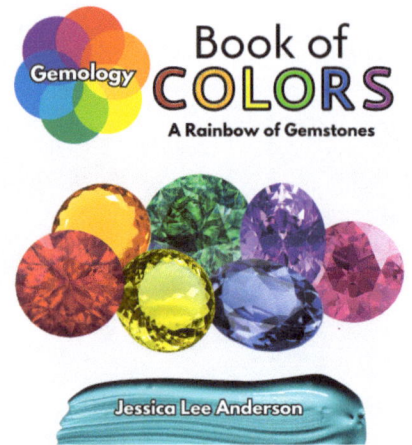

Herpetology
Book of COLORS
Nature's Rainbow of Reptiles and Amphibians
Jessica Lee Anderson

Ornithology
Book of COLORS
A Rainbow of Birds
Jessica Lee Anderson

Gemology
Book of COLORS
A Rainbow of Gemstones
Jessica Lee Anderson

www.ingramcontent.com/pod-product-compliance
Lightning Source LLC
Chambersburg PA
CBHW061145030426
42335CB00002B/106